AF409148

If you like this book and it helped you in some way or another, kindly post a review on Amazon.com.

HOW TO SURVIVE WORKING IN A CALL CENTER

So, you've accepted a role in a call center. Maybe this is your first time working on the phones. Or maybe you're a grizzled vet of customer service and you're looking for some tips. Either way, this book will help you. We're going to go over exactly what you can expect in your role, the different types of environments you might face, the individual challenges you'll face at a job-level and a managerial-level, and how to manage the stress (spoiler alert: yes, there's stress. Plenty of it.)

You'll almost certainly develop a cynical, sarcastic sense of humor if you don't have one already. Don't fret! This is a good thing. It can make bearing the job a lot easier if you can find humor in the things you're hearing from both management and callers on your line.

Before you trust me with your time, you're probably wondering what makes me qualified to give you this advice to begin with. Who am I, what have I done exactly that makes me so well-versed in call centers?

I've spent the majority of my career hooked up to a headset. I've worked all kinds of call center jobs—anything from billing, to insurance, and even technical support. I've been in enough of them to know the ins and outs. What's consistent across them, and what varies. If you read this book start to finish, you're going to have a better understanding of what the job is, what management's looking for, how you can keep your sanity, and what signs to look out for early on.

Without wasting any time, let's dive in!

CHAPTER 1: WHAT'S IN A CALL CENTER JOB, EXACTLY?

One of the things you might hear, particularly if you're in a billing role, is to "set the proper expectation." This could not be more true of any job itself, but a call center role in particular. After all, what does "call center job" even mean? Yes, you're going to be hooked up to a phone, but what then? Am I talking to companies or customers? Am I doing billing or tech support? Am I selling something or trying to de-escalate a situation? In some centers, you'll be doing all of the above.

If you've received a call center offer, you want to research the position. Internet research is great, but talk to people who are actually working the job if you can. Ask them about the good and the bad, see what the highlights of the jobs are, and the lowest of lows.

Ideally, even before you walk into an interview, you will have done some research on the position and you'll also have a feel for what to expect. Asking the interviewer is a great way to gauge things as well. While some will try to spin negative aspects into positive, most will be upfront about the position and what it entails. Companies have to spend money to train and prepare someone for a role, so they don't want to see you leave because nobody was honest about what the role consisted of.

To that end, during an interview, feel free to ask questions such as, "What is a typical day like in this role?" This will help gauge your day-to-day responsibilities. Some more open interviewers will go over all the types of calls you'll get—good and bad. From my experiences, when interviewers talk about negative aspects of the job, they're often better at preparing you for the role.

There are some pretty consistent items across all levels of call center as well. While there will always be exceptions to the rule, you can count on having to deal with someone who's pissed off at one point or another. I've worked call centers where this is every other call, and I've worked call centers where there was one of these every 5 months or so.

A lot of it is dependant on the role, but you're eventually going to talk to someone who unloads on you. More on that in the callers section.

The other thing you can count on is metrics. Call centers love to hold their agents accountable. Some are more flexible than others, but in general you're going to have a number or a series of numbers represent how you're doing to the company. Unfortunately, these numbers don't always correlate to how you're performing in the role.

We'll dive deeper into this under the management section, but at a high level, often times I've seen average handle time (how long you're on the phone), quality (are you saying what they want you to say), not available time (bathroom breaks outside of breaks/lunches, etc) and how many escalations you have as some of the more common metrics throughout my time in call centers.

The last thing you should consider is what type of company you're walking into. Is this a billion-dollar corporation? Or is it a local business barely on their feet? There's pros and cons to either.

Big companies aren't going to care about the little guy. You're a number, not even registering as a blip on their radar. Turnover is likely going to be high at these call centers because they can afford to staff more people, but at the end of the day most people don't want to work in a call center long-term.

Smaller companies are more likely to have your back, be more relaxed and care about you as the individual.Unfortunately, I also saw the dark side of this. When working for a tech support company, one of the service contracts expired and they let a guy go through no fault of his own, but simply because there wasn't as much money flowing into the company as before. These things happen.

Bigger companies will usually mean better benefits and more stability. If you're getting fired from here, more often than not it's due to a mistake you're making. Not to say you can't get screwed over—you absolutely can. But the odds of a big company tanking and firing you not due to job performance are substantially less.

Call centers will always vary. There isn't a universal truth. But I can guarantee you're going to eventually talk to someone who's pissed off, and I can also guarantee that the company is going to measure you in some way, shape, or form. Often times these metrics don't accurately reflect job performance, but centers insist on using them.

With that in mind, let's move on to dissecting what your first days will look like.

CHAPTER 2: WELCOME TO TRAINING

So, you've accepted a position and you're now going to start the long, tumultuous journey as a call center representative. Well done! Sort of. The first several days-to-weeks in a call center are nothing like the actual job. Don't expect to walk in day 1 and walk out the best rep on the phone. Don't expect to actually be on that phone for quite a while, actually.

Call center training is hit-or-miss. And I mean hard. Most have some standard training to complete in a classroom environment. One particular tech support role I had, this lasted all of 2 days. Others? 8 weeks. It all varies. I have noticed the larger the company, the more fleshed out the training seems to be.

Either way, you're going to be stuck in a classroom with a bunch of people most likely.

These days/weeks aren't the best. It's like orientation day at middle and high school, but for much longer periods of times.

Unfortunately, most companies seem to think it's a good idea to try and spice up the dry material with "activities" and "games". These are often juvenile and unnecessary, only adding to the boredom of the day. I've worked in centers where we gave presentations to the class like we were still in school. Others had us write answers to questions on paddle boards and raise them.

Expect to go back to high school for a few days to several weeks.

It's not all bad, though. While a lot of the training is going to be dry and even more of it won't help you in actual, on-the-phone scenarios, try to absorb it. If you don't understand something, ask. Don't fear looking like a dumbass, most people probably have a similar question.

You're going to pick up on other people in the class pretty quickly. If you're directly hired by the company, these people are your brothers and sisters, try to help them and form a relationship with them even if you don't like them. Some people will seem like they're miles ahead of you in knowledge, others might come off dumb as a rock. Either way, you're stuck in a small room with a lot of different personality types. Best to make the most of it. Never, ever start a conflict with someone else.

Some call centers also employ temp agencies before they hire you. These are worse: you're still stuck in a class with other people and need to remain cordial, but often times the company won't have spots for everyone and these folks are your competition. These jobs suck, to put it bluntly. You're often not viewed as a true employee until you're brought on permanent, you're not building up time off, you can't miss any days, and your pay is often significantly lower. Avoid unless you need the money.

Another thing: take notes. Write them down. Save them on your computer. But jotting things down is helpful. It's engaging, and it'll help with the dry material.

The trainers themselves are going to be a mixed bag. Some are good, some are bad. In many of the centers I've worked, you're going to have the trainer change throughout training, which sucks. But it can be good, also, if your trainer also sucks.

You'll be able to figure out their personality pretty quick. Are they cracking tons of jokes? Cocky? Dry, straight-to-business? You'll know what you have after the first day.

Same with the other folks in your class. Find people who are similar to you, try to be friends with them. Talk about things outside of work. You're there 8 hours minimum a day, might at least try to enjoy it a bit.

Eventually you're going to get to the part of training where you take phone calls. This is where the real fun begins.

Every center does this differently. Most have you paired up with someone else, be it someone in your class, or a senior rep who's been working the job. Some throw you to the wolves and let you fend for yourself.

No matter what, I promise you this: your first several calls will be bad.

Don't fret, this is fine. The company expects this, nobody thinks you will do perfect. This is the time to learn. Don't be afraid of making mistakes. Ask questions, either to more experienced reps, supervisors, your trainer, whoever. Get what you need.

However, do not ask the same question over and over again, nor guess what the answer is and potentially give out wrong information, or hang up on someone.

It's fine if you tell someone the wrong thing in training and then get corrected. That's a mistake and you won't make it again. But if the caller's asking about X and you've never even discussed/heard of X, put them on hold and clarify what the process regarding X is.

There's a fine line in call centers. Many preach "fake it 'till you make it." That's mostly true, but the other golden rule is, if you don't know, ask.

This training-but-taking-calls period usually lasts a few days to a few weeks. You'll be given crucial feedback about where you're excelling and where you struggle. Don't, under any circumstances, try to defend yourself against feedback from a superior. Thank them, ask them to elaborate on what they're seeing and how you can improve, and try to put it into practice.

One of the quickest lessons you'll learn in a call center is that making your supervisor and/or manager happy is going to take less stress off of you, even if they don't have you do things or say things you were taught in training.

Survive your training, and some centers throw a graduation party. Some don't. Either way, you're out of boot camp and onto the frontlines now. Welcome to a whole new world.

CHAPTER 3: POST-TRAINING/THE TRANSITION PERIOD

Well, you survived training. You've got some knowledge under your belt. You know what you're doing right and what you're doing wrong. You're still a newbie, but you've got some calls under you, you've got a feel for the job, you're doing alright.

At this point you more or less know what you've gotten yourself into. Every center has different metrics, different call volume—but you've experienced it. It's always best for a reevaluation at this point: now that you've worked the job, are you going to stick with it? You're probably coming up on your 90 day review period, if it hasn't already passed. You can always share concerns with management, but on a personal level, can you stick with this?

If so, read on.

Once you "hit the floor" (a fancy term call centers use for being out of training and on your own), it's a different ballgame. Yes, the calls are the same, but fatigue can really set in at this point. There's no more off the phone time. You're hooked up to that headset taking calls 8 hours a day or more.

Call volume and types of calls can affect how quickly you burn out.

If you're in this for the long hall, my first bit of advice is try to approach the calls with a genuine desire to help. Even if you're getting cursed out, try to show empathy even if they're being ridiculous. Call center work really just boils down to figuring out what that other person on the phone is doing calling into you. What do they want? And then, depending on what they want, giving them something as close to that as you can give them, or advising them of alternatives. More on dealing with this in the callers section.

At this point you likely have been assigned to a specific supervisor. You'll meet with them occasionally and review your progress. They're there as a resource, but some agents like to get close with their supervisor. This is ultimately up to you, though I caution restraint. Work is work, being buddy-buddy with a supervisor might get you seen and labeled as a kiss-ass and if that supervisor isn't liked by other folks, be it reps, management, etc you're going to be seen as an extension of that.

Do try to be friendly with your supervisor. Get to know them and what their experience in the company has been like. Continue asking questions, never stop building your knowledge.

We'll touch on supervisors more, and how to deal with bad ones, in the management section.

You'll quickly learn PTO and time off the phones are your keys to sanity. The daily grind will burn you out fast otherwise. I worked with a man who, as soon as he got his PTO, burned through it all by taking a week off. When he returned, we still had the majority of the year to go. He ended up quitting, and had to pay it all back. This is only applicable if you are at a job that gives you the PTO up front before you earn it, but do take note of this.

That being said, mental health days are a necessity. Do not be afraid to take them.

Off the phone time is different. This is for trainings, meetings, coaching, etc. One less-than-ethical thing I've seen people do is they get buddy-buddy with their supervisor and drag out their coachings. This, again, will get you labeled as a kiss-ass. Some other folks try this with trainers during training by asking a lot of obvious questions, etc. It's up to you whether you feel you want to employ these tactics. Off the phone time is valuable, but only you can decide if you'd trade looking like a dumbass to your peers for 10-15 more minutes off the phone.

You'll also be given a couple breaks and a lunch break. Some places have the option of not taking a lunch break and working straight through—that'd be up to you if you feel like powering through.

I recommend doing something completely different, far away from your desk. Go for a walk around the building. Listen to music. Browse the web. Play a game on your phone. Anything to break the monotony you've been subjecting yourself to. What I don't recommend doing is finding other employees and talking about, or bitching about work. Break and lunch time is sacred, and is to be treated as such.

When you're on the phones, many centers offer an option called "aftercall". This is where you can go into a different phone status and stop taking calls to finish notes, etc. This code is universally frowned upon. I've worked in centers where I could use it for 5 minutes at a time, and I've worked in centers where using it at all to avoid back-to-back calls would get you in serious trouble.

Sometimes you just need a break, but don't get in the habit of using it.

By now you'll be all-too-familiar with the systems you use every day. It's probably some antiquated computer program.

This will break. Sometimes often.

Unfortunately, call centers think it's a good idea to keep reps on the phone even when the systems aren't functioning. To that end, you're effectively answering calls and telling them you can help them with very general info, or they need to call back. Yes, it's stupid. But most centers require it.

I'm going to touch on call grading here as well, though that will also fall under management as we review your coachings. Every so often you'll have calls graded. A lot of the time your superior will want to listen to the call with you. This is always awkward, and a lot of times you'll have to grade yourself as well. Just do your best—no matter what, this is always weird.

Because call centers are high-stress, high-turnover, the staff often get things for free. Free lunches, perks, bonuses for working overtime, etc. Take advantage of these, they're one of the few good things about working in a call center.

CHAPTER 4: THE CALLER

Ah, the caller. You'll talk to plenty of them. Some you'll never forget —either because they're incredibly kind and understanding, or because they rip you a new one and verbally eviscerate you.

A lot of this depends on the industry you're working in. A lot of companies, particularly ones with large consumer bases, are naturally going to get more bad calls as people who are satisfied really have no reason to call in.

Businesses can be even tougher—you're not just talking to someone who's upset at one bill, it's a company demanding wage compensation for tens or hundreds of employees. Those conversations are not easy.

But before we dive in, let's scale back a moment. You'll only ever be talking to one customer/caller at a time, and that's the best way to view it. Try not to stress about a bad call that's either already happened, or is yet to come. Focus solely on the present, on the person on your line.

When you start deconstructing a call center job at a phone level, you're inevitably going to see some similarities. The longer you work the job, the more similarities you'll see. Maybe older folks who call in on your line have the same problem. Maybe a company policy in place is resulting in the same question being asked 10, 15 times a day and raising your call volume.

You can try to make mention of this to management, but a lot of time that won't help anything.

The main takeaway is that, in time, things will begin to feel familiar. This is good because you've gotten into a groove. You won't have to work as hard on the calls. You'll know the answer offhand. The downside is this can become incredibly mind-numbing over time.

Then, you have the opposite of this: the awful callers. The screamers. The irate. They go by different names, but it's someone who's pissed off at the world and they're going to take it out on you.

This will happen. At some centers, particularly those dealing with large amounts of money or in billing/collections, this is a daily, sometimes hourly occurrence.

So, how do you handle someone who's swearing at you? Screaming their head off, not letting you speak, filling your ear with all sorts of obscenities about how awful of a human being you are?

First, know your company policy.

Most larger companies aren't going to let you hang up on an abusive caller, which is bullshit but they're the ones signing your checks. Double-check company policy on this. Most are going to be something to the effect of placing abusive customers on hold and forwarding the call to a supervisor.

Whether you obey this or not is up to you, though I would caution restraint when dealing with an irate caller. Don't let yourself get emotional and hang up. That being said, there's a certain type of douchebag who will call in and make the call personal, insulting you and attacking you personally. I have no issue in saying I've hung up on these people in the past. They were few and far between, but at a certain point abuse isn't worth tolerating.

If this happens, it's up to you how to handle it. I forwarded all the call info to my supervisor, as well as the fact that the caller had been harassing me and using sexually vulgar language. I never heard a peep about it. Other people wouldn't say anything—they'd just keep going and hope management never noticed. It's riskier, but I've seen both ways work. One way, you're admitting guilt of breaking policy up-front and might suffer repercussions you wouldn't have otherwise. The other way, you're leaving it up to fate.

If you work for a smaller company, they will likely employ some sort of warning system for abusive callers. For example, if a caller swears 3 times and you've warned them already, you can end the call. Don't hesitate to employ this.

The golden rule here is this: follow policy. But there's another side to this as well.

Everything in a call center is recorded. Everything.

Mute is your friend. So is hold, but in my experience when on hold and not muted, quality assurance, your supervisor, and anyone else who listens to the calls can still hear you. So utilize mute. It's your best friend.

The last thing you want is for an irate call to spiral out of control and you start engaging the caller in a verbal war. That can get you written up and possibly fired.

The cruel reality is working in a call center means you're going to be a punching bag. That much is unavoidable.

To echo a previous sentiment in this book, every caller wants something. Some callers are calling just to complain and have someone to yell at. If you realize you've got one of these jerks on the phone, endure and move on. It's not always easy in the moment, but again: find what the caller wants, and deliver everything in the best way you can. Even if it's bad news.

You won't just get irate callers. You'll get some happy ones, ones who genuinely enjoy speaking to you. A lot of these are older folks who have nobody else. You'll also get emotional callers who cry. You can really just try to comfort them, no matter what they're going through.

There's the senior callers who call and have a hard time hearing you. There are ones who call and realize they called the wrong location, but might try to talk to you anyway. Sometimes you might get prank calls, mystery shopper calls, or ghost calls. There's no end to the different types. But if you handle each one one call at a time and focus on doing your best with each caller, the stress level will alleviate.

It's also important to recognize, as quickly as possible, if you can help a caller. You will get phone calls from people making absurd demands, or asking for things that you can't do. One piece of call center advice that does hold true is, "Don't dwell on what you can't do, tell them what you can do." So even if a caller is demanding something irrational, try leading with, "Mr. Customer, I apologize, but I can't do x for you. What I can do is ____"

Sometimes there's another side to that coin. Maybe you're working billing and someone can't make a payment. Maybe you're in insurance and someone thought something was covered when it isn't. When there's truly no alternative, nothing you can do in place of the bad news, be empathetic and focus on delivering the news with varying pitch in your voice and don't sound robotic.

Callers are a big challenge. They're the largest hurdle you'll have to overcome on the job. Some folks want answers now and are going to push back when you say you need to put them on hold to research something. Others are going to call in and demand to speak to a supervisor without giving you any information, even though company policy says you need to collect at least a vague idea of what the call is about before transferring.

The difficulties that callers will provide are endless. What's important is adapting to each call, doing what you can within policy limits, and above all else: focus on knowing what you can do for the caller as soon as you can.

The quicker you know what a potential solution might be, the quicker the call can be over.

Talk to senior reps. If your supervisor is relaxed, talk to them.

Learning is going to be your biggest asset. Ask questions, learn from every call.

Callers are the reason you have a job. A lot of times, they're the reason people leave call center jobs. Focus on doing what you can, be empathetic, and always try to be polite. Never be rude.

CHAPTER 5: MANAGEMENT

You'll quickly learn that callers are only one half of the equation. Management is the other. Management can be equally, or more stressful. They're grading you on tons of metrics. They'll come down on you for things outside your control. You'll be expected to hit certain numbers that don't seem feasible. And while some management is cool, many of them aren't. They're very business-like. But even that's fine. Other management will be vindictive, and some will seek to do your career harm if they're particularly bad.

In this section, we're going to talk about a lot of things. One of the first ones are metrics. I touched on this previously, but it's important to go in-depth on what these mean.

Metrics are how you're graded. If you're lucky, your center won't have any. I've been lucky enough to work in a center that has 1 metric, but never one that doesn't have any. These are out there, though.

So, if you're not lucky enough to land a call center job with no metrics, what can you expect?

- **AHT (Average Handle Time)** - This is how long you're on the phone. Not all centers manage it, but ones that do want you on and off the phone with the caller in a predetermined amount of time. Usually only in centers with a high call volume, as they want you wrapping up and moving to the next call.
  - Tip: Try to keep the callers focused. Some tend to let the conversations wander.

- **Quality** - This is how you're graded. This will be elaborated on by management, but suffice to say, you'll have certain things you need to do or not do during the duration of the call in order to meet a passing grade or score. Centers might have scripts, or specific lines they want you to say. You'll likely be graded on how enthusiastic you sound. Other centers grade you on responding to resistance and empathy. Usually your score is averaged out for the month and needs to be at or higher than the acceptable level.
  - Everyone grades calls differently. If your supervisor is grading your calls, try to get a feel for what they want to

hear and do it. Ask for specific examples.

- **Transfer Percentage** - I only worked in one center with this metric, but it was a very large company with many different departments. They advised us we should only be transferring a predetermined number of calls.
  - If this is a concern, if you can do even a shred of another department's work, do it to avoid a transfer.

- **Availability** - This is if you're on the phone when you're scheduled. I've seen it called adherence, availity, ready time, etc. Essentially just boils down to not taking additional breaks, coming in late, etc.
  - Try to be on time, that should alleviate any concern if you need an extra bathroom break, etc.

- **Aftercall/Not Ready** - Remember when I mentioned aftercall? Some centers track it. This varies wildly, from being allowed up to 5 minutes after a call, to none at all. This is one of the easier ones to slip up on, particularly if you have back-to-back calls. Try not to use it.
  - Take notes and finish any service forms required while on the call. It's often worth taking a hit on dead air for quality if it means using less aftercall.

- **Sales Rate** - My least favorite metric. Often, if you're a frontline phone rep for a large company with a consumer base, you'll be pushed (or required to, as per this metric) to make sales. Sales is a whole 'nother ballgame. But this metric can quickly mean pounds of stress. Try to avoid working in a center with this metric if you can, unless you're comfortable with sales.
  - Try not to position products as an ask only. Pair it with how it will help the customer. For example, adding an insurance to a phone plan might cost more, but if they're going through 2-3 phones a year, you're helping them save money in the long run. Explain this.

- **Escalations** - I only worked at one center that tracked this. Some centers believe you should be able to de-escalate most supervisor calls on your own, and will track (and possibly coach) you on how many escalations you have in a given timeframe.

- o Empathize and explain that there could be a long hold for a supervisor, and that you can take care of the issue now. Make sure they know what you can do for them, if anything.

That's all the metrics I've ever seen while personally working in a call center. I'm sure there are others, but these are the big ones.

Metrics can be difficult. If your center's strict, they're another layer of stress on an already-stressful job. Doubly so if you struggle with meeting one or more of them.

I really struggled with sales. I still am not great at them. I got coached on it many times. Your center may be different than mine, but what I can tell you is most call centers want their employees to succeed. The numbers might be unrealistic or difficult, but they're not created with failure in mind.

What does that mean? Well, if you fail to meet a metric, it's usually not the end of the world. They'll give you feedback, possibly let you shadow someone who's excelling at it to learn the tricks of what they're doing, etc.

If you continue to struggle with a metric, then disciplinary action happens. At one center I was at, after one month of not meeting a metric you got a warning, two months you got written up, three months you got a final warning, fourth month you were fired. At another center, they had one metric and I never got coached about it so they clearly didn't care. It's all about where you are.

Management will be off your back if you meet everything. But sometimes you don't, and management can be a real pain in your ass. More on that to follow.

As previously noted, it's fine to form lasting relationships with management. But keep it professional. Your boss has a boss, and their boss has a boss. Everyone's answering to someone. You want to fly under the radar, or have a positive image when people think of you. Nothing else.

So how do you deal with bad management at a call center?

It depends, but generally the rule will be "deal with it."

It's an unfortunate reality in any career that you might deal with bad management. It's luck of the draw. It depends on the company, culture, shift, etc. Some supervisors, managers, etc just plain suck. Some are too by-the-book and expect the world from you. Others are hired off the street and have no idea what it means to actually be on that phone at least 8 hours a day. Then there's the ones that are too laid back—cool people, but they don't do shit. All equally bad, all you will probably have to deal with at one point or another. If not at this job, potentially your next.

If you find yourself stuck in a position where you have a bad boss, flying under the radar will almost always be your best bet. Be friendly, do your work, go home. If you feel you're being unfairly targeted by your boss, larger companies have anti-retaliation policies. You should speak with HR at that point.

Bad bosses are a harsh reality of any career. Do your best to adapt to their style, focus on the money you're getting paid, and do your best.

Pleasing call center management can be a task like no other. Your metrics are only one aspect of it. Up next, we're going to look at attitude and presentation.

Everyone's going to take note of how you carry yourself. Are you late? Complaining to other coworkers? Are you pushing back when being coached on certain items? Are you causing escalated calls? All of this will be observed.

You're going to see other people bitch and complain about the job. That's the nature of a call center. Try not to partake—at a base level, negativity when you're already at work will do no good.

If management gets wind that you're unhappy, they might look for any reason to let you go. Numbers, attitude, I've seen management start pulling calls for those who are openly badmouthing the position. It's best to avoid this all together. Don't talk bad about the job, focus on your work, and don't waste another thought on it.

Common sense will reign above all. Despite the many different personalities, most call center management understands the realities of what you're facing all day.

Don't abuse the call out policy, don't piss anyone in management off, and meet your numbers. You should be fine.

CHAPTER 6: GENERAL ADVICE

Not everything is going to fall under a header like management or callers, so what else can you expect, and what other advice can I offer you?

- Offer to help out your coworkers, but only if they ask or you really see them struggling. If you know the answer and they don't, help them out. They might repay the favor.
- If given the opportunity to assist with a new training class, etc. Do it. It will look fantastic on your resume and can take a step towards progression. Progression means getting off that phone, and unless you love what you do that should be your end goal.
- You're going to see coworkers kiss ass and get additional time of the phone or move up because of it. Try not to let it infuriate you. This extends beyond call centers and is something you'll see at any job.
  - Tip: Don't become this person.
- Be cautious with PTO. I echoed this earlier, but be conservative in the first half of the year. You can be more liberal as the year winds down. Most centers reset their PTO in January.
- Calling in sick. Don't get used to it. Mental health days are fine, don't abuse them.
- Some centers allow shift swaps. Don't do these unless you can fully commit.
- Learn how to apologize. Apologize specifically for what the caller is asking that you can't do. Vary your pitch, sound empathetic. You will be apologizing hundreds of times a day depending on the center you work at.
- If your company lets you hand out credits on people's bills, don't go overboard. They catch wind of this, that privilege might be revoked and/or you may be written up.
- Sometimes you'll get callers complaining about other companies/etc. You're under no obligation to defend them, but just apologize that they had a negative experience and try to refocus the call.

- Find friends in the center. Genuine people you can trust. People who you can joke about and talk to outside of work. It makes life easier.

CHAPTER 7: LEAVING A CALL CENTER

So, you've put your time in. Whether you're moving into a new position in the same company, or you've gotten out of call center hell altogether, be happy. Breathe a sigh of relief. Your battle as a frontline soldier on the phones of war is coming to a close!

First, always put in a two weeks notice. Even if that other job calls you back and the thought of not taking another phone call has you salivating all over your desk, don't leave. Put in your notice. Be professional.

You want to leave the company on good terms. If, for whatever reason, your new role doesn't work out, having something to fall back on can mean the difference between making rent and eating, or being on your ass.

I turned down a job because I couldn't give my current center at the time two weeks, even though it was a fantastic opportunity.

Secondly, you can use this job as a reference. Two weeks guarantees that.

Your last two weeks after you put in your notice will be significantly less stressful. I will tell you upfront: it's fine to take it easy, but not at first. Spend your first week behaving like normal. Maybe if you have sales goals, don't worry about them.

In your last week, you can start to take it easier. These metrics won't matter after you're gone, but you still don't want to look like a tool who's showing up, going into aftercall for 8 hours a day and getting paid. It's just not worth it. Do your job, just be a bit more lax with yourself. Don't hang up on people, don't cause escalations, don't take several bathroom breaks or come back late. But taking some extra aftercall time, or not trying as hard on the calls you've breezed through before? This is all fine.

If you're sticking with the same company and transitioning into a different role, don't slack off quite as much.

Tell those people who have influenced and/or helped you that you appreciate their guidance. Thank your supervisor(s) for all they've done, even if you didn't always get along. Keep in contact with old coworkers.

Congratulations, you survived working in a call center.

CHAPTER 8: MAKING A CAREER OUT OF A CALL CENTER

So, maybe you don't want to leave the call center. Maybe the calls aren't as bad as you thought. Perhaps you're really good at it, and the monotony and repetition doesn't get to you. Or maybe you're good at talking to people and you're content with the pay. No matter what the situation is, if you want to make a career out of a call center, that's perfectly fine, too.

I would look at ascending the call center hierarchy. There's always the option of applying for a supervisor. You'll have a lot more responsibility, you'll be taking supervisor calls, and all the stupid things reps do to dodge calls will become your problem. But there's a nice pay bump (most are salary-based), you're off the phone for a good chunk of the day, and you get to see an entirely different side to call center work. You can see how all those metrics and numbers we spoke about earlier come into play.

The other thing you can do is remain on the phones and try to work your way up that way. Many positions have multiple levels. So there's, for example, Customer Rep 1, Customer Rep 2, etc. You'd want to speak to your supervisor about the requirements for moving up.

Much like becoming a supervisor, your knowledge will be expected to be high, and you'll need to be willing to handle more difficult calls. In some centers, this means starting to take escalated calls. In other centers, it means taking more complicated calls. It really just depends.

You can also see about transferring to a different department if you don't like the type of calls you're taking. For instance, if you don't like billing or collections, try tech support or sales. Just remember, each queue requires a different skillset. If you think you want to try sales because you're tired of talking to angry people on the billing side, be prepared: you're going to have sales numbers you need to hit every week/month. Same for tech support, you're going to need some outside knowledge of how phones, internet, tv, etc work.

If you're with a larger company, you'll probably get consistent raises with an eventual cap. The last thing you can do is just stay where you're at. No moving up, no transfers—just get damn good at your job and become one of the most knowledgeable reps. Keep getting your raises. If the calls don't bother you and you have no desire to move up, go for it!

CHAPTER 9: YOUR NEXT STEPS/FINAL THOUGHTS

Call center work isn't easy. I think everyone should work in one for at least a year. We'd have way less pricks calling in and treating us like trash.

But in the end, I'm not regretful of any of my call center jobs. They all taught me something valuable and kept me sharp with my customer service. Most had some interesting conversations with callers as well. There were always one or two calls, good or bad, I'll remember for the rest of my life from each one.

So, where do you go from here? That's up to you. I recommend settling into a role for at least a year before trying to move up. Take your time, get comfortable, get good at your job. There's always something more to learn, more you can do.

I hope you've found this book helpful in either preparing you for your first call center job, a refresher for someone returning to the industry, or a source of humor for those currently working in a call center

One thing you'll find is it takes a particular type of person to work in a call center. Mentally tough, willing to bare some of the worst that humanity has to offer. There's comradery to be found there. Learn about your coworkers, be friends with them. You're going to be doing the same job after all.

Thank you for reading this book. I hope you took something away from it.

www.ingramcontent.com/pod-product-compliance
Lightning Source LLC
Chambersburg PA
CBHW022011170726
47994CB00023B/3154